Autobiography of a Polybag

Rachna Khattar

ISBN 979-8-89067-897-3

Autobiography
— of a —
Polybag

Written & Illustrated
by
Rachna Khattar

Dear Children,
I am a shining blue, spotlessly
clean polybag. My parents
named me orb. I always wanted
to love and to be loved.
As you read through my journey,
in this book, you will learn more
about me and maybe you will
understand me, much more than
the world does today.

I was born from a small rubber ball in a shed. It was a polybag manufacturing factory.
There were so many like me.

I was proud of my shining smooth surface.
Whenever sunlight touched me, I would glow up.

One evening, we were packed into a bundle. The old man in the shed tied us up so tightly.
I couldn't breathe !

The following morning, we were handed over to a vegetable seller.

As the sun came up, mommies, daddies, grandma, and grandpa visited the cart to buy vegetables. One by one I started to lose all my friends.

Then a granny came to the cart. I was pulled out from the bundle and stuffed with tomatoes and chilies.

The chilies were naughty. They tickled me. Every time they tickled me, I would sneeze.

The tomatoes kept on juggling their places. One ripe big tomato squashed and the pulp just spread all over me, making me dirty.

When I reached grandma's house, grandma took out
all the vegetables. She washed and dried me.
I was happy to be neat again.

But my happiness was short lived. Grandma lined me up in the dustbin.

All day long vegetable peels, fruit skins, egg shells, leftovers kept landing into me. I started to smell bad. I felt unclean.

The next morning, I heard a loud honk,
followed by a song...

Swach bharat ka irada
Irada kar liya hai hamana......

Grandma lifted me from the bin, tied me up and handed me over to the garbage man.

The garbage man flung me into his dump truck and carried me off. There were many like me in the dump truck. Smelly, tied and bloated with household waste.

It was a bumpy ride. I could not keep my balance and fell off the dump truck with a thud, by the roadside.

As I lay by the roadside, a cow came sniffing upon me. I feared her broad teeth. She mercilessly tore me apart to eat peels and fruit skins.

Torn and lone, I just stayed by the roadside. Layers of dust covered me. My shine and glow were gone.

Motorbikes, cars, and trucks crossed over me.
I was crushed.

The wind carried me to places. I landed on a tree.

The tree swung its branches and shoved me away.

Birds pecked me and made holes in my body.

Once, I landed on an electricity pole.

The pole stood tall and mightly. It did not want a
poly bag around, so it started to heat up.
I started to melt and fell.

The city drains did not like me either. I would get stuck in some corner of the drain. The dirty city water would stop, and the drain would be full of smelly water. It would cough out loud and throw me out.

Whenever the winds were strong, many of us would be lifted into the air. I would hear people say," Oh! Look at those poly bags. So much plastic. Why don't we get rid of them".

By the roadside, I read a poster saying, "No to Plastic".

I also saw the symbol of 3R's

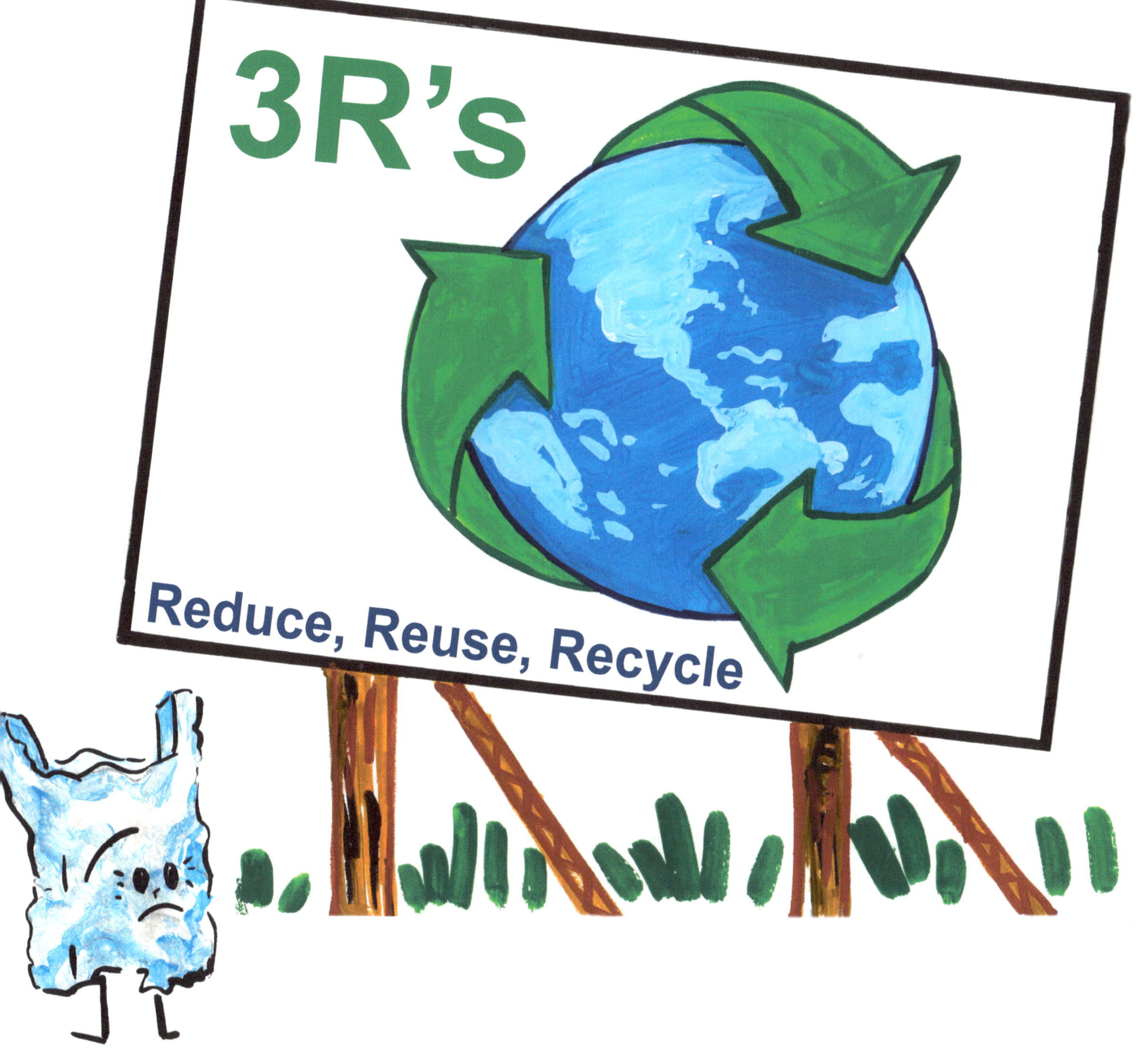

My friends and myself too wanted to save our Planet Earth. We all gathered for a green cause since Earth day was round around.

EARTH
DAY
APRIL 22

This Earth Day, I desired my own 3R's for every poly bag

On a beautiful sunny day, a ragpicker came to my rescue and many like me lying around.

She took us to a recycling unit where I would be recycled with other waste and made into a pot to hold blooming plants.

I finally got a better life where I will contribute to others' happiness. I would love and be loved. I got my 3R's.
I was Rescued, Reused, Recycled.